Economic, Government, and Reform Ideas for 21st century: Unique proposals to spur job growth, reduce debt, reform government, innovate, and restore trust in government.

By: Eric Wright
Twitter: @ericawright3170
email: ericawright3170@gmail.com
Author web page: http://www.amazon.com/-/e/B00HZEDQ6E
Feel free to check out all my self-published books. They include books on dating, mental illness, stress, coping, the Constitution of the United States, and on smartphones. They are also available on Kindle.

Thanks for reading and i hope you enjoy!

I0438252

Forward

I wrote this book because I am deeply concerned about America's future and the path that our government is taking. Our tepid economic recovery, our inability to work across the aisle with others to create millions of needed jobs, reduce our debt in a responsible way, and come up with ideas to continue to be a leader in the world and maintain our position as the top economic global power is troubling. The ideas i propose on government reform, job creation, and debt reduction are mostly original. You may love certain ideas and you may hate some, which is my goal to find bipartisan solutions that we all can get behind that nobody has every really thought of. I hope you enjoy the ideas enclosed and can pass on them so they have a shot at becoming law or you are in a position active in politics or lobbying and would like to better America's economy, create the millions of jobs that are needed, and help improve society for the better.

Economic Recovery, Gov't Reform, Debt Reduction Ideas

I. Taxes-

- End Bush Tax Cuts for the Wealthy. Return rates to what they were under President Clinton.
- Small businesses who make under $1 million a year and employ less than a certain number of people should pay a lower rate
- Businesses that manufacture goods in the United States should be rewarded a pay a low tax rate
- Reward Multinational corporations that hide money offshore and employ low wage workers in other countries by allowing them to bring back the money to the United States and not face a tax penalty if they hire more workers, increase wages, invest in new plants and equipment, and/or commit to keeping their money in banks owned and operated by the United States.
- Bush tax cuts for the middle class extended permanently
- Get rid of the estate tax
- Create a permanent solution to the Doc Fix, such as a standard national payment rate for Medicare doctors that automatically adjusts for inflation.
- Keep expanded Pell Grants for students
- Institute a payroll tax cut for employers by allowing them to receive a tax rebate equal to half of what a business pays in payroll taxes if they hire a new employee and keep them for at least 6 months or increase wages across the board.
- A 10 cent tax paid by bar patrons for every alcoholic drink purchased and a $1 tax on every carton of alcohol bought at a liquor store or vendor.
- Allow poll tab gambling at every bar and all profits made subject to taxes.
- Limit the number of deductions a taxpayer can take advantage of and percentage of one's income they can write off.
- Robin Hood tax of .5% on stock market transactions to help pay down the debt, invest in job creation, and stabilize the market.

- Find a way to get rid of the AMT (Alternative Minimum Tax) or patch it permanently so middle class taxpayer
- Allow taxpayers to deduct full cost of tax preparation. This will make sure that taxpayers receive the full amount of taxes back they deserve. It will also create jobs in the tax preparation industry. Counter this by having a agency that policies tax preparers, has random quality control inspections, and can take away the license of any business that does not perform correctly or rip people off.
- Continue to promote a progressive, fair, simplified tax code
- Allow anybody who is interested to donate money to the treasury to pay down debt or select an alternative where that money will go into a job creating fund.
- No tax deductions on second homes
- No tax deductions on yachts, planes for business travel, and other perks that are not necessary
- Institute a late filing fee for any tax returns that are not completed on time unless there is a good excuse accepted by the IRS.
- Produce a yearly report from the government that shows a detailed description of what the government spent money on and how much it costs to fund government programs.
- Tax Dividend, Capital Gains, and Carried Interest income as normal income
- No tax breaks for companies that ship jobs overseas. Have a government agency that produces a report of how much each company on the stock market earns, pays in taxes, how many people they employ, and where their workforce is.
- End Farm Subsidies for Multi-Million dollars farms
- Do not tax worker's tips

Notes/Comments Section

II. Election Reform Ideas

•<u>Invest in Safe, Secure, Efficient Electronic Voting Machines</u>. This will lower the voting lines at polls, speed up the election results. Have a competitive process to where companies can bid of creating the technology to be used across the United States. Once a company is chosen, you can have mock elections and a review process to insure the machines function properly and the government is getting a good deal and quality product for their investment.

•Have more early voting dates and times in every district. If need be, a person should also be able to set up an appointment to vote under the supervision of an election representative.

•All people should be allowed to vote early, vote via absentee ballot, etc.

•Every registered voter should have access online to a official sample ballot or be able to request a paper form so every voter is informed, knows who they want to vote for, and less time is spent at the polls.

•Every precinct should have a non-partisan individual available to take anybody who wishes to fill out exit polling data. Allow this data to wirelessly be submitted in real-time to the media.

•Have inspectors at every polling site to ensure that no voter suppression efforts are going on. If anybody is caught violating the rules, their ballot will be deemed illegal, face a penalty, and a suspension in their voting rights for a set time.

•Okay with ending contribution limits to candidates but all nominees must list their top donors and amount raised and have a chart listing how much of their revenue comes from all industries, businesses, special interests, and committees.

•Every political commercial must disclose who is funding the ad

•Cut down on organizations that file as a non-profit whose main goal is to influence policy

•Institute term limits for all Senators of 3 terms (18 years) and 12 years for representatives.

•Count all early voting Ballots beforehand and keep under lock and key to ensure that the final result is correct and handed down swiftly

III. Immigration Reform

*Pressure the House of Representatives to take up and vote on the Bipartisan Senate Immigration Reform Bill that passed with 67 votes or take up the Republican Alternative that the House as offered, and if needed, go to conference and work out the differences.

Some Ideas that could be incorporated in the Bills are:

•Continuing to build and patch more fencing along the border and add more checkpoints if economically and geographically feasible.

•Stop spending money on high-tech fencing that has consistently malfunctioned.

•Invest more money into increasing the number of Border Patrol agents, add more drones and surveillance along both borders.

•Create more centers across the country that are designed only to monitor the drone activity so there isn't a huge backlog of data that hasn't been looked at.

•Train and enlist more drug sniffing dogs at checkpoints and those that can assist agents patrolling the border.

•Allow the United States government to sell drones to our allies and countries abroad that need the technology if it is in our National Security interest.

•Institute a National ID card that contains encrypted info on a person's criminal history, qualifications that will show if one is legally able to work in the U.S., fingerprint data, or anything useful to make sure that justice is served and police have all the resources they need on the job.

•No tax breaks or "magnets" for illegal immigrants or those with temporary Visas/green cards unless they sign documents stating they will start to learn English, pay a fine, always file their taxes or attend a credited college, serve in the military, etc.

•Pass Dream Act

•Peope who were brought here when they were young and: maintain a clean criminal record without major drug offenses, violent crimes, or federal convictions, as well as finish a high school/college degree should not have to face criminal charges, be deported, or face exhorbant fines.

•We must have one national law and not a patchwork of different immigration laws by the states. It only makes the job for immigration officials more complicated and inefficient. It also can be confusing to any immigrant or employer looking to hire.

•Have a 1-800 number hotline for illegal immigrants or those going through the citizenship process. If they need advice, help, or any information about citizenship, deportation, the status of their case, or any other matter, the call should remain anonymous unless a national security threat gleaned from the call must be acted upon.

•Increase port security and make the scanning of all freight and containers more efficient. All containers must be inspected when arriving and leaving and should be tracked accordingly. The sooner they fix this problem and find a way to accomplish this goal, the better.

IV. Energy Independence and Policy Reforms

•Allow more offshore drilling. All oil companies and refineries must be inspected frequently and have many backup safety plans in case of an oil spill.

•Explore and open new areas for natural gas drilling. Studies must be done to determine the effects of fracking on the environment and a person's health. Victims who have suffered health consequences from fracking should be able to sue for damages.

- Crack down on unfair trade, currency manipulation, and clean energy practices by China.
- Continue to allow U.S. manufacturing companies to take advantage of production, equipment, and development tax breaks.
- A 10% corporate tax rate for all U.S. manufacturers.
- All start-up and established businesses should have loan and credit guarantees if they meet certain criteria.
- Homeowners who choose to have an inspection done of their home that will advise them of any potential issues, how to use less energy, make their homes more efficient, and lower their monthly bills should receive a tax credit.
- No tax break for oil companies unless they can prove that losing their tax breaks will raise prices dramatically for consumers or force them to lay off many workers. If an oil company continues to receive tax breaks, they must come up with a written plan on how they can lower their operating costs, reduce the wholesale price of gas, and continue to maintain a profitable business without laying off workers.
- Set reasonable emission standards for plants, factories, and power companies. If the business is compliant with these regulations, they should be rewarded with a tax break. If they don't pass the quality control standards, they should receive two warnings with information on how to meet them. If afterwards there isn't a concerted effort to comply, they should be assessed a penalty determined by a national standard and based on the company's assets.
- Support reduced car insurance rates for those who own or upgrade to a hybrid, electric, or other vehicle with a high MPG rate.
- Tax breaks for homeowners who update to energy-star qualified appliances, install solar panels on their homes or businesses, or install a green-friendly landscape.

•Promote donation of old vehicles to those who are poor and needy. People who donate should be eligible for a tax deduction.
•Vote down the Keystone Pipeline project because of the environmental damage building it will cause as well as the lack of permanent jobs that it creates and most, if not all, the oil will be going to foreign countries and not dramatically reduce gas prices here in the U.S.

V. Personal Debt Reform

•Eliminate a person's student loan debt after a certain number of years paying on time and is in good standing.
•Institute a policy to elimate any student loan balance of a person who gets a degree in a highly desired and important field like science, engineering, teaching, medical after a certain number of years.
•Allow bankruptcy courts to wipe out all of a person's student loan debt if it is determined that they can't afford to pay it.
•Reduce student loan interest rates
•Allow students to pay student loan amount based on a percentage of how much they earn.
•Promote credit counseling services
•All banks should provide a free credit report at request of a customer.

- Bankruptcy courts should be allowed to lower a person's mortgage principal if their house is determined to be underwater and/or this decrease will allow the homeowner to stay in their home and not have the bank foreclose on it.
- Crack down on internet "get rich quick" schemes by allowing the president and regulators to shut down any site that grossly overpromises, commits fraud, and is not a legitimate form of employment.
- All personal and government debt of any person who dies must be cleared and the living relatives should not have to be harrassed or forced to pay any of the deceased debts.

VI. Violence and Gun Policy
- Reinstitute Assault Weapons Ban
- People should not be allowed to bring any type of weapons into National Parks or on trains and any type of public transportation.
- Any Handgun or semi-automatic weapon with the capacity to hold more than 12 bullets should be illegal.
- Invest in after school programs for all students. All kids should have a place to stay and do homework, exercise, socialize with peers if a parent isn't home or their environment isn't safe.
- Every school should have workshops on self-esteem. Even a casual seminar where students can discuss their problems and their lives with other peers would be great.
- All schools should have bullying seminars and support groups for those who feel teased, unloved, and all alone, etc. This will help those being bullied and going through rough times to know that they are not alone and so students can relate to each other more. I believe the atmosphere of schools will significantly improve if you follow some of these steps.

•All gun purchases must be entered into a database with ballistics information, serial numbers, and the owner's information as well as the gun's past. This will help law enforcement solve violent crimes easier and improve safety for all americans.

•Gun safety classes and training should be required for all handgun purchases.

•Background checks at gun shows and every transaction involving a gun must be required. People convicted of stalking, violation of restraining orders, domestic abusers should not be able to purchase a gun without the court or psychologist signing off.

•Institute a program to give free gun locks out to every gun owner.

VII. Medicare Reform

- Free STD screening and counseling on safe sex and mental health assistance for those afflicted with an STD.
- Slightly raise Part D premiums for disabled people
- Crack down on medical providers and other people who approve of scooters for people who get around just fine and it's medically proven that they don't need them for their well-being, being productive, and safely getting around.
- Means Test Benefits
- Make what is covered easier to understand. Provide a hotline for those with questions and cut down on the wasteful paperwork and documents sent each year.
- Continue and expand coverage for wellness programs like free or discounted gym memberships and at-home workout kits
- Cover all approved smoking cessation programs.
- Give checks or another form of reward to people who attend better health seminars or local community education classes.
- Continue to cut down on medical fraud. Have an online database where the government inserts data everytime a physician approves certain prescriptions or services. If regulators find that certain doctors overbill Medicare or constantly and recklessly approve of medical procedures that aren't necessary, that doctor or medical facility must pay the government a hefty fine and/or lose their right to be a Medicare provider.
- Pass Medical Malpractice and Tort Reform. All doctors must not have to worry about going out of business if they tried to do the right thing but make an honest mistake. In addition, the amount a plaintiff receives in such cases should be limited and a cap placed on the total amount one can be awarded based on the injury and seriousness of such.
- Allow the government to bargain with drug companies to receive better prices.

•Allow drug re-importation from Canada. Also have one site where consumers can review any source they bought medication from and the government can warn of unsafe drugs.

•Allow people looking for health insurance to buy policies from across state lines.

•Slowly increase Medicare eligibility age only if necessary.

•Allow pharmacists and doctors to run a check of what vaccinations and/or shots a patient is qualified for, covered by their insurance provider, and is medically appropriate.

•Continue to promote generic medications

•Medicare should provide a monthly newsletter talking about techniques to better one's health, how to notice if you are experiencing potentially bad symptoms and what to do about it, as well as inform medicare beneficiaries of any service that may prolong their lives, make them happier, and reduce their healthcare costs.

•Invest in free health clinics in inner city and rural areas where there is a need for quality care that is affordable and doctors that specialize in certain areas of medicine.

VIII. Social Security

•Make paychecks easier to understand. Workers should be able to know what the taxes that are taken out of each paycheck are being used for.

•Lift the Payroll Income Tax Cap to $250,000 a year or more. The wealthy should pay more in payroll taxes and of course be able to recuperate most of that money when they retire.

•Means Test Benefits. If you don't need social security, maybe you could have the option of donating your benefits to reputable charities or go into a state fund that can be used to hire the unemployed.

•Reduce backpay amounts to no more than $10,000 unless the recepient has a large outstanding medical, student loan bill, or any debts that need to be paid back.

•Chained CPI cost of living increases for all recepients of social security.

•Streamline the filing process for disability and suggest people do their business online.

•Increase the incentive for disabled people to work, if they choose and are able to do so. You can do this by deducting from their Net income after taxes and not the Gross Income. Also allow them to pay the same in prescription and premium costs. Social Security should also pay for the full cost of employment training, provide a one-stop website for companies to list open jobs that the disabled may find appealing, and reassure those worried about losing benefits if they find that they aren't able to hold down their job.

•Free copies of certified death records.

•Get rid of the $250 social security death payment. I just think that it is wasteful and offensive because it doesn't even come close to covering the costs of funerals.

•Evaluate all disability applicants for any chemical dependency issues that may be the reason why they can't hold down a job and come up with a plan to help them spend their money wisely if approved for benefits.

•Focus on keeping people in homes. Expand foster care. Give monthly payments to those who choose to stay home full-time to care for their aging and sick loved ones.

•Allows PCA's to bring their clients grocery shopping and pay them for mileage driven.

•Every year send out documents that show how much a worker has paid in taxes, earned at each job they have held, and estimated monthly benefits they would receive if they retire.

•Payroll tax cut for businesses that hire the disabled and veterans.

IX. Infrastructure

•Use 1/4 of parking fines collected for sidewalk repair, 1/4 for infrastructure repair, 1/4 for new and easy to read road signs, and the rest used for debt reduction and investing in new innovation and technology.

•Rent out or sell unused private/public lands to build golf courses, parks or recreation areas, or build and create new businesses, residential areas if the owners and government agrees.

The owners of private privaty would be able to receive a lump sum and royalty payments.

- Invest in a new smart power grid
- Help all airlines install GPS flying radars to increase efficiency of flying and reduce accidents. All airlines after a certain number of years should be required to have said technology.
- Pass a Highway Bill similar to the one Former congressman Jim Oberstar of Minnesota lobbied hard for.
- Continue and expand tax breaks for electric cars, gas stations or businesses installing charging ports, wind turbine manufacturers, and solar panel sellers.
- Invest in high speed Rail
- Have emergency phones along every busy Interstate or Highway
- Fines for repeat Hitchhiking violators.
- Have a ridesharing program in as many areas as possible where people can carpool with other safe and certified drivers.
- Lower speeding fines. Have a progressive speeding penalty for repeat violators.
- Every highway or road that has any danger or unsafe landscape on it, must have a guardrail.
- Have monthly required and random inspections of roads and bridges. Have the DOT come up with a standard grading system. If a bridge, road, or any infrastructure fails or needs work in certain areas, the applicable state should receive a notice to repair the problems. All road projects and any documents showing needed repairs should be transparent, subject to congressional oversight, and all interested parties should be able to read the reports and weigh in on the matter.
- Have a dedicated site where drivers can air their grievances, comments, and/or complaints on the quality of infrastructure like bridges, roads, etc. that need to be repaired or addressed.
- Invest in the Army Corps of Engineers
- Incentivize internet service providers to build and expand fiber optic and broadband internet across the U.S. All low-income,

disabled, and elderly should be able to receive a monthly credit if they qualify under income standards.

•Require all Infrastructure projects to use Made in the U.S.A. products unless they are not available or too expensive to buy.

•Give funding to state and local government to buy more street cleaning and sidewalk sweeping/clearning machines so that pedestrians and motorists have the best possible conditions to get around.

•Install more lighting along roads

•Fine repeat jaywalkers with no exceptions, unless there are no useable crosswalks and signs in the area.

•Make sure all interstates, highways, and roads have a bigger shoulder to pull over on.

•All street lights should stay green, yellow, and red for the same amount of time period.

•Have signs next to the street light that shows how many seconds to red so there are less drivers that run red lights.

X. Sin Tax-Alcohol, Gambling, ETC

- 10 cent tax on all alcoholic beverages purchased in bars and a $1 tax on every carton of alcohol bought at any liquor or grocery store.
- Allow gambling online and in Bars, but an individual should only be able to spend or bet a certain amount of money each day. All winnings from gambling, poll stabs, and other bets are automatically subject to taxes taken out.
- Video game tax on games that don't get you moving and burn calories.
- Pay sales tax on all junk food items purchased

XI. Health Policy

- Gived insured a reward each year for undergoing a physical with lab test.
- Promote the idea of employers giving bonuses to employees who meet certain health goals that are mutually agreed upon.
- Allow visits to a Nutritionist for $0 co-pay

- Expand hotlines where a concerned person can call a certified nurse or doctor and discuss symptoms to determine if it is the person's best interest to go to the doctor or emergency room.
- Keep track of people who repeatedly visit Emergency Rooms and provide consultations to see how they can better improve their health.
- Cover self-esteem and body image improving classes.
- Again, we need more anti-bullying and cyber bullying support and programs.
- Every student no matter their grade, should be able to have recess time to get some fresh air and exercise.
- Provide a $100 check to overweight and obese people who watch the documentary "Fat, Sick and Nearly Dead" and come up with a plan to change lifestyle and eating habits.
- Improve and make the Food Pyramid chart more readily available.
- All restaurants must list the nutritional information on the menu board or have the information easily accessible to anybody interested.
- Use video game sin tax to help fund community recreation programs, healthy living classes, and organizations dedicated to fighting childhood obesity, diabetes, high cholesterol, and high blood pressure.

XII. Education Policy

- Teach budgeting and financial responsibility to students.
- Tax credit and assistance for schools who institute or expand high-tech in the classrooms.
- Lower the number of standardized tests. Allow teachers to teach to their student's ability and not to what the government thinks a kid should know at a certain age.
- Have teacher evaluations every year that are standard across all schools. Every teacher who meets or exceeds goals, should receive performance pay.
- Make sure students have easy access to affordable and healthy food choices, including breakfast.
- Allow businesses who are looking to hire have a class where eligible people who complete the requirements be offered a guaranteed full-time position.
- Every class junior high and up should have a syllabus
- Offer free tutoring at school or online covered by the state.
- If parents choose to enroll their student in a private or charter school that costs money, they can receive a check covering the average public school's education costs per student.

XIII. Animal Rights

•Increase penalties for animal cruelty violations

•Help support local humane societies and adoption places.

•Crack down on puppy mills. All buyers should be given information on how the puppy was raised, where they were born, and learn about the conditions that they lived in before buying.

•Have clear penalties and consequences for anybody choosing to own dangerous and exotic animals.

•Offer advice and information on how to properly care for the animal that you buy.

XIV. Judicial Reform

•Metal Detectors at every courthouse. Make sure their are armed officers and judges in every building.

•Expand the people who can be put in contempt if they are being disrespectful, disruptive, and/or not answering questions.

•Pay a penalty if you do not show up for your court date.

•Speed up the Judicial Process. Hire more public defenders. Combine different elements in the trial that are related. Have a maximum number of times that a case can be continued.

•All people convicted of any crime or on probation/parole, must submit a sample of their DNA and have pictured taken and entered in the appropriate databases.

•All Supreme Court cases should be televised, unless congress and the President agree that for national security reasons, it should not be aired on national television.

•All people convicted of a crime and imprisoned should be allowed to take a DNA test if they request to prove their are innocent.

•Reform the Death Penalty. Make sure lethal injection drugs work effectively and are carried out in a humane way. Speed up the amount of time between a person's conviction and death by execution. Only the most heinous of criminals like serial, spree, or child killers and people convicted of a hate crime should be subject to execution.

•Provide financial and counseling help to families of convicted felons to try and help break the cycle of crime and reduce the recidivism rate. It will also help the whole family move up the economic ladder and have more of an opportunity to pursue their dreams.

XV. Illegal Drug Policy
•Get rid of mandatory minimum sentencing.

- Reduce the number of alcohol and cigarette advertising.
- All alcohol and cigarette products must be behind the counter
- For drug crimes, try to focus on mental health and economic issues that may have lead an individual to use drugs, instead of automatically sentencing them to prison.
- All college athletes should be able to receive endorsements and get paid as long as they keep their grades up and pass random drug tests.
- Regulate, Legalize, and Tax Marijuana and Hemp use and production
- Invest in more K-9 Units
- Make sure that all freight at our nation's ports is scanned and documented to improve our national security and help weed out illegal activity.
- Shut down black market drug dealing sites.
- People should be able to go to the police and seek treatment for a drug addiction problem without facing the legal consequences.
- Have the Scared Straight program in every county.
- All DUI offenders must pay for and install a device in the car that measure their BAC in order to start the vehicle.

XVI. Housing and HUD Reform
- Tax deduction for all apt building that have or install security features or increase their energy efficiency.

•All apartments that have a certain percentage of units that fail inspection should lose their ability to be section 8 certified unless they fix the issues in a reasonable time.

•Promote the idea that all apartments have meetings to address concerns, activies to meet fellow residents, and even a volunteer team to help clean the building and report issues so residents develop a sense of pride and responsibility.

•Have a Section 8 rent calculator online with average apt. prices, the maximum rent that a family can choose, and a link to where all section 8 landlords can post listings and people searching for a apartment can view their options.

•Streamline the application process so one doesn't have to be on the waiting list for a long time.

•Have less paperwork to fill out and more of the application and investigation process done online.

•Be allowed to mail in or fax documents and have a phone interview, instead of being forced to take the day off work and find a ride to the appointment.

•All areas should have legal aid and a hotline where landlords and tenants can go to resolve any disputes.

•Each tenant must have a pamphlet that clearly discloses the resident and landlord's rights, responsibilities, and talks about the appeal process, and what needs to be met to having a safe and sanitary living environment.

•All recertification and application forms should have clear instructions or a booklet that discusses how to fill out said forms.

•People who face eviction should be able to have a judicial hearing where a judge and jury of one's peers can determine if they were evicted fairly.

XVII. Washington Reforms

•Have seminars and events with representatives and politicians to try and get people involved in politics or help guide people looking to work in government

•All congressman should have a website that lists all of the bills they have introduced, how they have voted on all issues, etc. so voters can great a accurate idea of their performance.

•Lower the number of nominations by the president that are subject to votes

•Streamline the budget process and have the proceedings more transparent.

•Reform the filibuster

•Everybody should be able to email a politician's chief of staff and receive a response if needed.

•Have early voting everywhere

•Charge money for visiting attractions in Washington D.C.

•No anonymous blocking of bills. Representatives must write a statement of why they oppose the bill and/or address congress and the nation.

•Have a site where people can go to to see a sample ballot

•Allow representative should receive a secure email and cell phone.

•Politicians must vote on every issue in person or by email, text, message or online. If they don't, they will face a penalty that is higher the more important the bill is.

•Anybody who donates big money to a politician should be forbidden from receiving an ambassadorship or any political job just because of supporting them.

•Electronic Voting in the Senate

•Put in place term limits for all representatives and Senators

•Take money out of politics. Repeal Citizens United with a constitutional convention.

- Lessen the time that senators debate a bill, unless both parties agree that more time is needed.
- Every bill that comes before the Senate must be able to have a certain amount of amendments voted on. These amendments must be an equal amount Republican and Democrat.
- Politicians must work more each year or have their pay reduced.
- Have fines for disruptive behavior on the House or Senate floor.
- All representatives and senators must sit together at the State of the Union with their colleagues from across the aisle.
- Every person running for election must publicly disclose their big donations and how much money they receive from certain industries.
- Congressman must post who visits their office just like the White House.

XVIII. Food/FDA
- Allow mystery shopping of all businesses.

•Provide a reward to vendors and stores that choose to accept EBT/SNAP cards.

•Food stamp recepients should be allowed to buy hot food, but it can be taxed.

•Promote the idea of politicians living on food stamps for a month.

•Have bigger and clearer food labels.

•Speed up production of medications.

•Doctors should have a site where they can review studies, success rates, and reviews of medications that they want to prescribe.

•Have public ad campaigns for healthy living.

•Have a study on how to produce more food safely, naturally, and with less chemicals

•Have a born-on date for all food.

•Grocery stores should have a easily accessible fruit and vegetable section and list the benefits that each provides.

XIX. Jobs Ideas

•Have a summer jobs program for High School students.

•President must appoint a council of economic advisors that he meets with regularly. The committee can consist of business leaders, politicians, and activists that can provide some fresh

ideas on job creation, innovation, smarter regulation, and any measures he may be interested in lobbying for congress to pass.
•Any employer that hires an unemployed person and keeps them for atleast 6 months, should get a payroll tax cut.
•Create a fund to help states hire firefighters, police, and teachers.
•Special grant for students who choose to study science, medicine, or engineering.
•Have a special label for products made in the U.S.A. or are produced in an environmentally friendly manner.

XX. Healthcare Reform
•Require all government employees to purchase health insurance through the exchanges.
•Reduce the level of income that qualifies for a subsidy under the Affordable Care Act.
•Promote the idea of a public option.
•Purchase insurance across state lines.
•Tort Reform
•A public monthly unbiased report on how the law is doing.
•Online website to post any idea that can be voted on and the President must respond.
•Online medical records

XXI. Bills I Approve Of

- Pass the Senate's postal reform bill to help save the post office.
- Pass Rand Paul's TSA Reform Bill
- Pass Immigration Reform
- Pass a Comprehensive Energy and Climate Change Bill to create jobs and reduce our dependence on foreign oil.

XXII. Miscellaneous

- Post all bills online and in Lehman's terms.
- Stop funding National Academy of Arts
- Invest in more vending machines that accept credit cards.

•Require monthly press briefing by the president and suggest more meetings between the president and representatives.

•Have the opposite party of the President post a response to the Weekly Address if desired.

•Rent unused office space, vacant buildings, or land for parties and events to help fund the state and local government and help create jobs.

•Tax deduction for people who regularly ride public transit.

XXIII. TSA Reform

•More explosive and drug sniffing dogs at airports.

•Hire more behavioral analysts that look for suspicious behavior.

•No fees for carry-on and checked luggage.

•Screen all fliers before boarding against the no-fly list and any wanted fugitives.

•Have new planes with a map of world and GPS locator showing where the plane is, how fast it is traveling, etc.

•All flights must have an air marshal on board.

XXIV. Medicaid Reform

- Reduce overpayments to hospitals.
- Cover contacts exam for no or a small fee.
- Give a discount to people who choose to get LASIK eye surgery.
- Cover Dental Services.
- Expand Medicaid access in every state.

XXV. Law Enforcement

- Give incentives who prove that they are good at proactive police work, adopt a community policing philosophy, and police departments that actively track crime stats and look for ways to improve.

•Have a plain clothes liason that any citizen can go to with concerns about their community.
•Have an easy to access free public records search
•Have a pysch evaluation for most criminals. Focus on rehabilitation and mental health treatment.
•Be able to text 911
•Have a standard number to call for non-emergencies.
•Focus on restorative justice. Require more convicts to volunteer.

XXI. Foreign Policy
•All military action must be approved by congress.
•Reduce foreign aid to every country and offer them trade deals instead.
•Leave all foreign bases that are not needed. Reassign all of the laid-off troops to other bases or offer them free job training, a college education, and/or other financial assistance.
•Debrief all congressional members on foreign policy goals and what is going on in the world.
•Put restrictions on U.S. businesses who do transactions with anti-U.S. countries.

XXII. Some more pay-fors

- sell gold that is stockpiled and invest in job creation and reduce debt.
- sell rare coins and government items online
- Sales tax on clothing purchases.
- Fee on driver's license renewals/registration.
- Fuel Tax
- Fee to sign up or transfer utility service.
- Higher penalty for youth smoking
- End NASA trips to foreign planets
- Have competitive bidding process for all military equipment.